Maui Travel Guide

2023-2024

Simple and Quick Way to Experience the
Real Maui as a Courageous Traveler -
Discover the Hidden Gems and Vibrant
Culture

Nathan Campbell

Table of Content

PART I: Introduction

Welcome to Maui

Welcome to Maui, a tropical paradise that promises an experience that will be unlike any other. The little Hawaiian island of Maui is renowned for its breathtaking landscapes, immaculate beaches, and rich cultural heritage.

When you arrive, the islanders will greet you and make you feel at home with their kind aloha attitude. From the moment you step foot on this stunning island, you will be immersed in a world of magic. Maui's diverse topography offers a variety of options for outdoor enthusiasts, wildlife lovers, and folks who want to unwind.

Take a look inside the legendary Road to Hana, a magnificent journey via lush jungles and gushing waterfalls. Discover the magnificent Haleakala National Park, where you may see the dawn from the peak in wonder. The best way to absorb the island's cultural history is to take part in ceremonial events and sample local food.

Maui has stunning beaches where you may bask in the sun and a wide range of thrilling water activities. Enjoy luxurious resorts for a relaxing getaway or the laid-back charm of local communities. The duration of your stay on this lovely island paradise is certain to be filled with adventure, peace, and cultural immersion.

Welcome to Maui, a location where the aloha spirit and the beauty of nature join together to create an experience that will live forever in your heart. Get ready to travel for a lifetime and create treasured memories in this idyllic tropical setting.

About this Guide

Hello and welcome to the comprehensive "Maui Travel Guide," which was written to be your closest companion while you explore the delights of this magnificent Hawaiian island. Whether you're visiting Maui for the first time or are a seasoned traveler, this guide is intended to enhance your enjoyment and help you get the most out of your vacation.

In these pages, you'll find a gold mine of precious information, insider tips, and expert recommendations that will assist you with every part of your trip. Everything from creating an itinerary to locating hidden jewels is something we can assist you with.

Our team of passionate travel writers and residents has laboriously put together this book to provide you with the most up-to-date knowledge on Maui's most popular attractions, lesser-known hidden treasures, and unique experiences. You can depend on the information you find here to be accurate, current, and a good representation of the geography of the island, which is always changing.

What to Expect

Discover in-depth Maui's gorgeous beaches, well-known locations, and breathtaking natural treasures. Investigate the fascinating location's fascinating history, lively culture, and diverse customs.

To give your vacation to Maui a unique twist, learn about hidden treasures, off-the-beaten-path activities, and local favorites.

Practical Advice: From travel alternatives to budget tips, we provide essential information to assist you in organizing a seamless and pleasurable vacation.

Dining and hotel: Indulge in the island's culinary specialties and choose housing that meets your preferences, whether you're seeking luxurious resorts or more reasonably priced options.

Safety and Respect: We emphasize ethical travel practices and guide in preserving Maui's sensitive ecology and appreciating its rich cultural history.

We want to help you develop a close relationship with Maui and its people, create precious memories, and open yourself up to new experiences. So, grab your sun hat, buckle in for an adventure, and let the "Maui Travel Guide" lead you on a tour across paradise you won't soon forget.

Why Visit Maui?

With its enticing attractiveness, the island of Maui, popularly known as the "Valley Isle," lures tourists from all over the globe. Every visitor should include Maui on their bucket list for a variety of reasons, including the magnificent scenery and the vibrant local culture.

Beautiful Natural Scenery: Maui is a veritable paradise with some of the most breathtaking scenery on the planet. Watch the dawn while standing atop the dormant Haleakala volcano, where ethereal colors dance across the horizon. Examine the legendary Road to Hana, a beautiful path that goes through lush woods, gushing waterfalls, and uncharted beaches. Explore the West Maui Mountains' wild splendor or relax on beautiful beaches while the Caribbean Sea laps at your toes.

The Culture: Accept the warmth of Maui's culture, which is characterized by the spirit of aloha. The island's rich tradition is celebrated via ceremonies, captivating hula shows, and captivating storytelling. Create an authentic and immersive experience by conversing with hospitable people who are ready to share their customs.

Outdoor Activities: Maui is a haven for outdoor enthusiasts and nature lovers. Snorkelers may see beautiful sea turtles and a variety of vivid fish as they explore the colorful coral reefs. Surf at popular spots or pick up stand-up paddling in sheltered coastal waters. Set out on thrilling excursions through verdant valleys to enjoy hidden waterfalls and stunning views.

Whale watching: During their annual migration, the majestic humpback whales may sometimes be seen in Maui. From December to April, these gentle giants frolic in the warm Hawaiian waters, producing magical moments as they breach and sing their beautiful sounds.

The food: Take part in a delectable gastronomic journey on the island. As you experience the many tastes of the Pacific, savor traditional Hawaiian cuisines like Lomi-Lomi fish, poi, and delicious kalua pork. The farm-to-table movement on Maui guarantees the use of fresh, locally sourced foods, enhancing the eating experience.

Wellness and Relaxation: Rejuvenate in the serene atmosphere of Maui. Enjoy luxurious spa treatments, practice yoga in picturesque locations, or just relax on a tranquil beach while being calmed by the sound of softly breaking waves.

Sunsets to Remember: Sunsets are a magnificent way to finish the day, illuminating the sky with hues of orange, pink, and purple. Whether you're seated in a hammock by the coast or perched atop a cliff, Maui's sunsets are a sight to see.

From cultural vultures to adventure seekers, Maui caters to all of their demands. Its seductive charm, extensive history, and boundless natural beauty come together to create an experience that is beyond expectations. Pack your luggage, show some aloha, and go on an unforgettable adventure to Maui, the magical island.

PART II: About Maui

Geography and Climate

Maui, the second-largest Hawaiian island, is a fascinating patchwork of diverse terrain and microclimates that is hidden away amid the Pacific Ocean. This appealing locale offers a fascinating mix of scenery, including stunning volcanic peaks, lush jungles, and undeveloped coasts.

Volcanic activity millions of years ago sculpted Maui. The two primary volcanoes that predominate the island are Haleakala, a dormant shield volcano that creates the eastern section of Maui, and the West Maui Mountains, an eroded shield volcano that produced the western part of the island. The beautiful Haleakala Crater, a caldera at Haleakala's peak, is a must-see for its unearthly landscape.

East Maui Rainforest: As the trade winds traverse the island, they encounter Haleakala, which causes them to rise and chill. As a consequence, the eastern slopes of the island are covered in lush rainforests. Along the Hana Highway, which meanders through this tropical wonderland, you may find a secret waterfall, bamboo woods, and unusual vegetation.

The middle valley of Maui: This is a small isthmus between Haleakala and the West Maui Mountains. This lush region's patchwork of agricultural fields is home to a variety of crops cultivated on rich volcanic soil, including sugar cane, pineapples (which were previously a large industry), and other crops.

West Maui Mountains: The West Maui Mountains are both rocky and lush, which makes them stand out dramatically from the rest of the island's geography. With its tough paths and stunning scenery, this area is a hiking lover's paradise. It features high cliffs and deep valleys.

The coastline: It is stunning, with lava-rocked shorelines, white-sand beaches, and spectacular sea cliffs. From the well-known Kaanapali Beach to the secluded and unspoiled beauty of the Nakalele Blowhole, each length of coastline has its charm.

Climate

Maui has mostly tropical weather, with a few small geographical variances. The western and southern beaches of the island are normally dryer, but the eastern and northern parts of the island have more rainfall.

Summer (May to October): Warm and dry, with average highs of 88°F (24°C) and lows of 75°F (24°C) throughout the summer, this peak tourist season is ideal for beach and aquatic activities.

Winter (November to April): temperatures normally range from 68°F to 80°F (20°C to 27°C), with a little bit more rainfall. It's also the best time to go whale watching since humpback whales are migrating to Hawaii's warm seas.

The year-round beautiful weather on Maui is made possible by the trade winds, which provide a refreshing breeze.
Embrace the island's varied terrain and friendly environment as you discover Maui's natural beauties, go on thrilling excursions, and immerse yourself in the splendor of this tropical paradise. No matter whether you're

swimming among bright coral reefs or viewing the dawn from Haleakala's peak, Maui's topography and environment provide the perfect backdrop for an amazing encounter.

History

The history and culture of Maui are just as varied and interesting as its scenery. This fascinating island has been shaped by encounters with colonial powers, centuries of Polynesian tradition, and modern influences. As we investigate the interesting past and present of Maui, take a journey through time.

An ancient Polynesian community
Long before European explorers arrived, Polynesian mariners explored the wide Pacific Ocean and discovered the Hawaiian Islands. Hawaiian oral legends attribute the discovery of Maui and the establishment of the modern-day Hana area to the mythical explorer Hawai'iloa. The early immigrants who came to the island with their customs, languages, and spiritual beliefs laid the

foundation for the unique Hawaiian culture that is still here today.

The kingdoms of Maui

By the 15th century, the Hawaiian island of Maui had been divided into several chiefdoms, each with its head of state. The most prominent chiefdoms are Hana, Wailuku, and Lahaina. As a consequence of these chiefdoms' competition with the adjacent islands, conflicts and alliances regularly occurred.

The arrival of Captain James Cook

When British explorer Captain James Cook arrived in the Hawaiian Islands in 1778, it marked the beginning of serious interaction between the islands and Europeans.

The presence of Cook piqued the interest of the Hawaiians while also upsetting them.

Sadly, his entrance not only brought alien illnesses but also resulted in a significant number of native deaths.

The Hawaiian Islands' union

King Kamehameha I, a capable diplomat and warrior, began an endeavor to unify the Hawaiian Islands in the late 18th century. After effectively unifying the islands under his rule by military force and clever alliances, he founded the Kingdom of Hawai'i in 1810. As the political and cultural center of this confederation, which encompassed Maui, Lahaina played a prominent role.

The Lahaina whaling industry's boom

Due to the whaling business, Lahaina had a significant inflow of foreigners throughout the 19th century, transforming it from a sleepy town to a bustling port city.

The presence of whaling ships from all over the globe in Lahaina's port led to a colorful mix of cultures in the city.

The iconic banyan tree in Lahaina, which was planted for the first time in 1873, is still recognized as a shining example of this era.

The Arrival of the Missionaries

Early in the 19th century, Christian missionaries arrived and converted the Hawaiians to Christianity. Although their presence drastically changed Hawaiian religious customs and traditions, they contributed to the preservation of the Hawaiian language and the advancement of education.

The Dissolution of the Hawaiian Monarchy

Political instability resulted in the collapse of the Hawaiian monarchy in the late 19th century. Businessmen from the U.S. Queen

Lili'uokalani, the last reigning queen, was overthrown by a government-organized coup in 1893 with aid from the U.S. Hawaii was later acquired by the United States in 1898.

Hawaiian culture in the modern era.

In the 20th century, Hawaii had a cultural renaissance known as the Hawaiian Renaissance. The goal of Hawaiians and their supporters was to revive the traditions, languages, and artistic expressions that had been suppressed under colonial administration. Hawaiian culture is celebrated and preserved thanks to this continual comeback of identity and culture.

Ka honua

Appreciation for the natural world, is a fundamental aspect of Hawaiian culture. The ancient traditions of hula dance, chanting (mele), and storytelling have continued to uphold the spirit of aloha down the years. The concepts of "ohana" (family) and "lokahi" (unity), which establish links throughout the community, are at the core of Hawaiian ideals.

linguistics and education

The Hawaiian language, which was once in danger of extinction, has undergone a comeback as a result of measures to integrate it into educational and cultural projects. Hawaiian language preservation for future generations depends on schools offering the language as a second language.

Festivals and Celebrations

Maui has a wide variety of intriguing cultural festivals and events throughout the year. Annual Maui Film Festival, Makawao Rodeo, and the Maui County Fair are just a few of the occasions that showcase the island's rich cultural legacy and creative talent.

Maintaining natural and cultural resources

More people now understand the importance of preserving Maui's natural and cultural treasures in recent years. Traditional fishing methods are being restored, holy places are being conserved, and the island's sensitive environment is being safeguarded.

Modern-day Maui

Modern Maui is a harmonious fusion of local customs and outside influences. Its colorful culture is influenced by the island's multinational population, which consists of

Hawaiians, the offspring of early settlers, and immigrants from Asia, Europe, and the US mainland.

Tourism in Maui
Annual visits by millions of visitors to Maui have a major economic effect. Although the tourist industry has benefited the economy, efforts are still being made to balance it with sustainable practices to preserve the island's unique personality and natural beauty.

As a result of these extensive ties, Maui's history, and culture have helped to create a reputation for the island as a haven for aloha, natural splendor, and cultural riches. While warmly embracing visitors from throughout the globe, the people of Maui continue to preserve the lokahi spirit.

By learning about the island's history and present, visitors may make a lasting imprint on their hearts and minds and connect with the soul of Maui. Good day, and welcome to the eternal embrace of Maui's past and present.

Local Customs and Etiquette

When visiting Maui, it's crucial to respect the local way of life. Respecting local traditions not only encourages friendly interactions with residents but also makes it possible for you to get a real sense of the Hawaiian way of life. Here are some helpful hints on how to act correctly and respect local traditions when traveling:

The Aloha Spirit, which emphasizes treating people with compassion, love, and respect, is the cornerstone of Hawaiian culture. Be courteous, and thoughtful, and treat others with warmth and sincerity to embody the aloha spirit.

When welcoming someone, a cordial "aloha" (hello) and a warm smile go a long way. The "honi," a traditional Hawaiian greeting that includes delicately touching foreheads and noses while inhaling, may be used in addition to the standard handshake by locals. However, the majority of relatives and close friends behave in this manner.

It's usual in Hawaii to remove your shoes before entering someone's house. This courteous gesture respects the host and helps to keep their houses tidy.
In Hawaii, particularly close to the ocean, there is a casual clothing code. However, it is important to wear modest clothing and proper footwear while visiting public spaces, restaurants, or activities.

Respect for Holy Sites: There are several historical sites and temples in Hawaii that are regarded as holy. Never touch or disrupt these regions; always be respectful of them. Any issued guidelines or warnings should be followed.

Honoring Kapu (Taboos): Be aware of any kapu (taboos) associated with certain places or activities. For instance, some regions could be subject to limitations or off-limits hours according to cultural conventions.

Cleaniness: The purity and cleanliness of their island are treasured by the Hawaiians. Always dispose of rubbish appropriately and keep an eye on the environment.

Mahalo (Thank You): Express heartfelt thanks by saying "mahalo" when someone is helpful or offers to help. Thank yous are an important component of Hawaiian culture.

Photography: Be courteous and ask people's permission before taking photographs of them, particularly during events or gatherings.

Respect for Local Wildlife: The wildlife of Hawaii, both on land and in the water, is unique and should be seen from a distance. Avoid touching or upsetting marine creatures when snorkeling or swimming.

Attend Fairs: Learn about local customs and traditions by taking part in cultural activities like lei-making workshops, hula performances, and other such events. The history of the island is illuminated by these meetings.

By following these local customs and etiquette, you will not only show respect for Maui's culture but also deepen your bonds with the community. Unquestionably, if you embrace the spirit of aloha and immerse yourself in the local traditions, your stay in Maui will be improved.

PART III: Planning Your Trip

Best Time to Visit

The island of Maui explodes with vivid hues and blooms throughout the spring, signaling a time of rejuvenation. Between 70°F and 82°F (21°C and 28°C), the weather is still nice and good for a range of outdoor activities. While wandering through stunning, in-bloom landscapes, discover Maui's verdant gardens.

The island hosts the Maui County Agricultural Festival every year in April, when visitors may taste regional food, discover traditional agricultural methods, and go on farm excursions. Surfers from all over the globe go to well-known breaks in the spring because of the ideal surf conditions that are available.

It seems to reason that the summer is Maui's biggest travel season. Visitors may take advantage of the island's beautiful beaches and water sports any time of year since the island's average annual temperature ranges from 73°F to 85°F (23°C to 29°C). Learn how to paddleboard while standing up, go snorkeling in the pristine sea, or just unwind on the sandy beaches.

Local performers and foreign films are shown outside during the Hawaiian Slack Key Guitar Festival and the Maui Film Festival, respectively, every year in June and July. Take part in cultural activities and let your creativity soar

On Maui, autumn is a quieter and more laid-back season. This time of year is perfect for outdoor activities like trekking and visiting Maui's waterfalls and rainforests since the average temperature varies from 70°F to 83°F (21°C to 28°C).

September marks the month-long Aloha Festivals, a celebration of Hawaiian culture and tradition that includes parades, concerts, hula shows, and artisan fairs. A fantastic chance to interact with people and discover what aloha means.

Generally speaking, your interests and the sort of experience you're searching for will determine the ideal time to visit Maui. Maui welcomes visitors all year round, whether they want to go whale watching, take in thrilling festivals, enjoy the ideal beach weather, or just unwind.

Any time of year is a good time to visit this tropical paradise since each has its special beauty. Grab your sunscreen, buckle in for an adventure, and let Maui's natural beauty, unique culture, and spirit of aloha captivate you.

Traveling to Maui

Visitors may get to the Hawaiian island of Maui, a tropical paradise, in several straightforward methods. Accessing Maui is now simpler than ever, regardless of where you are traveling from inside the United States or internationally. The following are the most current means of transportation to get to this beautiful island.

Trip to Maui

Kahului Airport (OGG), which is located in Central Maui, is the primary airport servicing the island of Maui. Direct flights to Maui are available from a large number of locations in the United States and other countries on several major carriers. From major hubs including Los Angeles (LAX), San Francisco (SFO), Seattle (SEA), and Honolulu (HNL), regular flights are offered, according to the most current information.

Flights between islands

Inter-island flights are a practical method to get to Maui whether you're already in Hawaii or wish to visit other islands. Numerous airlines provide regular flights between Honolulu on Oahu and Kahului on Maui. Island hopping is straightforward since most flights are between 30 and 45 minutes.

cruise vessels:.

Cruise ships that often stop at the Hawaiian Islands typically visit Maui. Passengers on cruise ships have the option to take shore excursions and see Maui's coastline when they arrive at Kahului Harbor or Lahaina Harbor.

You may take a ferry to Maui from the nearby islands of Lanai or Molokai for a more exciting experience. Between Kaunakakai, Molokai, Lahaina, Maui, and Manele Bay, Lanai, there is a ferry service. Because they may change, double-check the ferry availability and timetables.

Private vessel charters
Reserve a private charter or air taxi if you like a more individualized and sumptuous travel experience. You may choose your timetable and take in the breathtaking aerial vistas of the Hawaiian Islands with a private charter.

When you get to Maui, you may explore the island at your leisure using shuttles, city buses, and rental automobiles. Make travel plans, pack your luggage with sunscreen and beachwear, and get ready to fly to Maui to enjoy its natural beauty and welcoming culture. Maui is a destination that guarantees lifelong experiences.

Visa and Entry Requirements

To guarantee a simple and trouble-free journey, it's critical to comprehend the visa and entrance criteria if you're considering visiting Maui, a lovely Hawaiian island. The following information about Maui's visa requirements and entrance regulations is current as of the most recent changes.

U. S Citizens

if you're an American citizen. Americans may go to Maui and the rest of Hawaii. nationals of the U.S. who are visa-exempt.

Hawaii is a state of the union, thus citizens of the United States can visit and live there without a visa. To board your aircraft and enter the nation, you must have valid government-issued identification, such as a driver's license or passport.

The following items are covered under the Visa Waiver Program (VWP).

You may travel to the United States, including Hawaii, for business or pleasure if you are a citizen of a nation that participates in the Visa Waiver Program (VWP). According to the most current data, travelers from VWP nations must first apply for an ESTA. For up to 90 days, immigration without a visa is permitted thanks to the ESTA. Make sure to check the most updated list of VWP nations, and get your ESTA approval well in advance of your travel.

Non-VWP Nations

You need visa if you're a citizen of a nation not covered by the visa waiver program.

Keep abreast of the most current entrance and travel restrictions because of changing political climates and official mandates. For

the most latest and accurate information, visit the US government website.
There are websites for the Hawaii Tourism Authority and the Department of State.

Before your vacation to Maui, make sure to prepare ahead and have all the required paperwork and permissions. You may discover the natural splendor of this tropical paradise, learn about its culture, and encounter the welcoming aloha attitude of the residents. You may anticipate a wonderful and delightful vacation there with the proper preparation. Safe travels on your trip!

Travel Budgeting Tips

Many individuals believe that a vacation to Maui would be the ideal escape due to the island's breathtaking beauty and fascinating culture. But if you want to truly enjoy all the island has to offer without going over budget, you must make the required travel arrangements. To help you get the most out of your Maui journey, consider the following helpful travel budgeting advice:.

Research and Plan

Plan a thorough schedule before leaving and research the price of any related flights, lodging, and activities. To save money, look for specialty discounts, sales, and seasonal specials. Making reservations in advance is another excellent strategy to save lots of money.

Create a Realistic Budget

Decide on your spending limit when creating a budget for your vacation to Maui, and then allocate precise amounts for items like travel, hotel, meals, activities, and souvenirs. Spend your money sensibly and give your most significant experiences high attention.

Traveling Off-Peak

To avoid the peak travel season, think about visiting Maui in April and May and between September and November. You may dodge the crowds and pay less for flights, hotels, and activities during certain periods.

Choose Accommodations Wisely

Find a location to stay within your limits by looking into numerous choices. Think about booking an inexpensive hotel, hostel, or vacation home. If you want a more opulent experience, seek for discounts on expensive resorts when they're less crowded.

Plan your trip with care, embrace the spirit of aloha, and let Haleakalā's majesty leave a lasting impression on your heart and soul.

Safety and Travel Tips

The Valley Isle, generally known as Maui, is a tropical paradise filled with natural marvels and cultural pleasures. If you want to ensure a pleasant and safe holiday, it's essential to be well-prepared and aware of safety measures and travel advice pertaining to this beautiful Hawaiian island. Whether you're a seasoned traveler or a first-timer, these tips will help you make the most of your vacation to Maui while prioritizing your health:.

Keep an eye on the sea
Tourists are drawn to Maui's stunning beaches and crystal-clear seas, but it's crucial to appreciate the power of the ocean. When snorkeling and participating in other water activities, be sure to snorkel in lifeguarded areas, look out for rip currents, and take all necessary safety measures. Consult

trustworthy tour companies or locals for advice when in doubt.

Sun Protection

On Maui, the tropical climate guarantees a year-round supply of sunlight.

Your skin will be protected from harmful UV rays by wearing a wide-brimmed hat, sunglasses, and sunscreen with a high SPF. Keep hydrated and seek shelter at the height of the sun's rays to avoid sunburn and other heat- and sun-related problems.

Ocean Wildlife

The seas around Maui are home to an abundance of fascinating marine species. Keep a respectful distance from the coral reefs and other marine life while swimming or snorkeling since they are vulnerable and protected. During the whale-watching season, which lasts from December to April, schedule a guided excursion to safely see these majestic animals.

Honor the environment and the people.

Maui's lush Hawaiian culture is intertwined with its beautiful natural surroundings. Respect holy places, don't trash, and stay on the approved pathways to reduce your environmental effect. Learn about local customs and participate in cultural events with respect and understanding while adopting the aloha spirit.

Weather Awareness

The weather in Maui is prone to abrupt fluctuations, especially at higher elevations like Haleakala. Pack layers of clothes so you can adapt to temperature variations and be prepared for intermittent downpours. Check the weather and the condition of the roads before embarking on an expedition, particularly if you want to visit Haleakala National Park or the Road to Hana.

Driving Safety

If you're renting a vehicle in Maui, be cautious, particularly close to Haleakala and the Road to Hana. Drive sensibly and cautiously, and pull over when necessary to allow quicker traffic to pass. Watch for one-lane bridges and, if required, yield to incoming vehicles.

Protect Your Priceless Items

Although Maui is typically secure, it's crucial to always keep your valuables locked up. Never leave your valuables unattended when at the beach or in a rented vehicle. Hotel safes should be used to store vital papers, money, and passports.

Carry Snacks and Water

While experiencing Maui's natural splendor, be hydrated by carrying a refillable water bottle. Bring refreshments with you on hikes and excursions, such as energy bars, bananas, or local delicacies.

Making Sensible Financial Choices

Budget carefully since Maui may be expensive. Look for grocery shops, food trucks, and happy hours to get inexpensive meals. Take advantage of cheap or free activities like beachcombing and hiking trails.

COVID-19 considerations.

Observe the COVID-19 guidelines that apply to Maui. Please be aware that laws may change for the sake of your safety as well as the protection of the community. Be flexible and mindful of local rules as a consequence.

Travel Insurance.
Consider purchasing travel insurance to safeguard your investment from unforeseen disasters or trip disruptions.

Emergency Preparedness
Find out who to call and what to do in an emergency. Save important phone numbers, including those for the neighborhood emergency services, your hotel's front desk, and the consulate or embassy of your country.

By following these safety and travel tips, you'll be well-prepared to take in Maui's delights and create treasured experiences that will last a lifetime. Embrace the aloha attitude, be aware of the island's natural and cultural assets, and let Maui's beauty and friendliness win your heart throughout this amazing experience.

PART IV: Attractions in Maui

Haleakalā National Park

The picturesque Haleakala National Park in Hawaii attracts visitors from all over the globe to the island of Maui. For both nature lovers and adventurers, the park's 33,000 acres of varied terrain, rare flora and animals, and spectacular vistas make it a must-visit destination. You just need to be aware of the facts provided here to understand Haleakala National Park.

A geographical wonder

The eastern shoreline of Maui is formed by the huge shield volcano Haleakala, whose name in Hawaiian means "House of the Sun." The park's height at the Haleakala Visitor Center is 10,023 feet (3,055 meters), and it completely encloses the volcano's peak. The top region is usually referred to as the "crater" despite having a massive depression known as a "caldera."

Sunrise and sunset displays.

The top of Haleakala is famed for its views of the sun rising and sunset. The sun rising above the clouds, which paints ethereal colors across the sky, draws tourists who get up early. Sunsets, which are equally enthralling owing to the shifting colors that paint the landscape, are a stunning example of nature's beauty.

Hiking trails

For hikers of all skill levels, Haleakala National Park offers a variety of hiking paths. From short, strolls to challenging multiday hikes, the paths, such as the Sliding Sands Trail, Pipiwai Trail, and Halemau'u Trail, lead hikers through stunning scenery. A permit is required for backcountry camping, so it's crucial to have the necessary equipment on hand, including enough water.

Unique flora and wildlife
The park is home to a wide variety of plant and animal species, some of which are exclusive to this region of the globe. Keep a look out for the native silversword plant "Hina Hina," which blooms only once in its lifetime and is a unique sight to witness. You could observe the nn, sometimes referred to as the Hawaiian goose, which is the state bird of Hawaii.

Stargazing
Due to its dark sky, Haleakala is a fantastic site for stargazing. The park has been recognized as an International Dark Sky Park, allowing visitors to see the Milky Way and innumerable stars in the night sky. To make the experience better, ranger-led activities and stargazing events are offered.

Visitor Information Centers

The summit-located Haleakala Visitor Center and the park's coastline Kipahulu Visitor Center are the two visitor facilities in Haleakala National Park. The centers' enlightening information, displays, and ranger activities will enhance your awareness of the park's geology, history, and conservation efforts.

Weather and clothing

At Haleakala's peak, the temperature regularly gets below freezing at night, making it much colder than it is at sea level. It's important to dress in layers and be ready for quickly changing conditions. Additionally, it's a good idea to pack water, sunscreen, and sturdy shoes for hiking and other outdoor activities.

Entry fees and authorizations

There is a three-day admission charge at Haleakala National Park. If you plan to visit other national parks in the United States within a year, think about buying an America the Beautiful pass, which grants access to all national parks and federal recreation grounds.

Sunrise viewing and reservations

Due to its popularity, reservations are essential for a dawn viewing from Haleakala's top. Both tourist management and environmental protection are aided by the reservation procedure. Due to its popularity, reservations for dawn viewing should be made much in advance.

Environmental Stewardship

Haleakala National Park's sensitive ecology necessitates the protection of its delicate environment. Follow Leave No Trace guidelines, stay on authorized paths, and don't scare off any plants or animals. Please heed the warnings and directions presented to protect this natural gem for future generations.

A representation of Hawaii's spectacular natural beauty and extensive cultural heritage is Haleakala National Park. No matter whether you're stargazing beneath the clear heavens, traversing the trails, or watching the dawn from the peak, a trip to Haleakala is sure to be an amazing and illuminating experience.

Iao Valley State Park

With its magnificent beauty, historical value, and peaceful atmosphere, Iao Valley State Park is a beautiful natural marvel that draws tourists. It is situated in Maui, Hawaii's gorgeous surroundings. This 4,000-acre state park is a must-visit place for anyone who enjoys the outdoors and wishes to fully appreciate the island's rich cultural legacy. Information about Iao Valley State Park is given below:.

A geographical wonder
Iao Valley State Park is located in Central Maui, around 4 miles (6 points 4 kilometers) west of Wailuku. The centerpiece of the park is the imposing Iao Needle, a 1,200-foot (366-meter) high peak that abruptly rises from the valley floor. The West Maui

Mountains feed the Iao Stream, which in turn creates a serene panorama of emerald foliage.

Iao Needle

The most famous building in the park is the Iao Needle or Kuka'emoku in Hawaiian. Because it is such a stunning natural feature, Hawaiian culture considers this sharp, lush pinnacle, which was created by centuries of erosion, to be holy.

Historical Relevance

Iao Valley has significant historical and cultural value to the Hawaiian people. The terrible Battle of Kepaniwai took place there in 1790 when King Kamehameha I attempted to unify the Hawaiian Islands. In the end, he won the battle and cleared the path for Kamehameha's reign to unify the islands by defeating the Maui leader Kalanikupule's army.

Ethereality's beauty

What makes the park so lovely is its ethereal charm, with its mist-covered summits, bright rainforests, and a plethora of tropical vegetation. The lush valley vistas are evidence of Hawaii's varied ecosystems and unique microclimates.

Hiking trails

Iao Valley State Park offers a variety of hiking paths with varied degrees of difficulty. The Iao Needle Lookout Trail is a short, paved path that leads to an observation platform with expansive views of the needle and the valley. For those looking for a lengthier experience, the Iao Valley Stream Trail provides a lovely stroll along the stream with opportunities to explore native plant species and cool waterfalls.

Cultural Preservation

It is strongly advised that visitors respect the park's cultural value to the Hawaiian people. Stay on approved pathways, respect the valley's spiritual and historical value, and don't harm native vegetation.

Climate and Dress

Because the weather in Iao Valley may vary fast, it's crucial to be prepared for shifting conditions. Remember to pack clothing for chilly days and use suitable hiking shoes. Don't forget to use bug repellant and sunscreen as well.

Accessibility

The Iao Needle Lookout Trail and the park's parking lot are both accessible to those with limited mobility. Before beginning longer walks, it is essential to evaluate the accessibility and route conditions since alternative paths may have more challenging terrain.

Park amenities and hours of operation.
Iao Valley State Park is accessible every day from sunrise to sunset. Along with bathrooms and picnic sites, the park has a visitor center where you can learn about the natural characteristics and history of the valley.

Environmental Stewardship
You may respect the park's delicate environment by adhering to the Leave No Trace rules. Don't trash or do anything else that could damage the environment or cultural landmarks.

Visitors may interact with Hawaii's rich legacy and fully experience the island's stunning scenery at Iao Valley State Park, a refuge of natural beauty and historical importance. If you visit Iao Valley State Park, whether to gaze at the Iao Needle or hike the valley's paths, you can expect a tranquil and illuminating experience that will leave a lasting effect on your heart and spirit.

Wailea Beach

Wailea Beach, a gorgeous and undeveloped stretch of shoreline that offers guests a traditional tropical paradise experience, is located on the southwest coast of Maui, Hawaii. Wailea Beach is renowned for its golden beaches, clean seas, and lavish resorts. It is a refuge for leisure, water sports, and stunning sunsets. The information below about Wailea Beach is all you need to know.

Location
Wailea Beach is located in the posh resort area of Wailea, which is just south of Kihei. Thanks to its advantageous position, upscale hotels, great restaurants, championship golf courses, and high-end shopping are all conveniently close by.

Stunning Scenery

The beach is unparalleled in beauty with its smooth, golden sands reaching down the coastline, lush, well-kept gardens, and swaying palm palms. The Pacific Ocean's stunning deep blue color provides the beach's background.

A family-friendly setting.

Wailea Beach is ideal for groups of all ages and families traveling together. The mild surf and gradual entrance into the sea make swimming, wading, and even novice snorkeling safe activities there. Lifeguards are on duty during the busiest hours, adding an extra layer of protection.

Water Sports

Diverse water sports may be enjoyed in the calm, clear waters at Wailea Beach. Snorkelers may explore the underwater environment that is populated by brightly colorful fish, turtles, and sometimes even manta rays. Other well-liked activities include stand-up paddleboarding, boogie boarding, and kayaking.

Beachside facilities

For the ease and comfort of guests, the beach includes several facilities. With bathrooms, showers, and picnic sites readily available, it's easy to take advantage of a day in the sun without compromising comfort.

Spectacular Sunsets

Wailea Beach is well known for its stunning sunsets, making it the perfect place to relax in the evening. A wonderful background for enchanting strolls down the coastline is created by the reflection of the hues of the sky on the water's surface.

Quality resorts and spas

Wailea Beach is surrounded by some of Maui's most luxurious hotels and spas.

Guests may create a memorable and opulent holiday by indulging in spa services, gourmet cuisine, and five-star lodging.

Shopping

At the adjacent Shops at Wailea, which provide premium shopping, you may find a range of shops, art galleries, and fine dining establishments. Watch the sun fade over the horizon while sipping beverages or enjoying dinner while admiring the water.

Accessibility and Parking

Parking spaces are nearby, making it convenient to travel to Wailea Beach. Visitors staying at the neighborhood resorts may stroll to the beach since there are several homes with direct beach access.

Protection of the environment

Keeping Wailea Beach's natural beauty intact requires responsible tourism.

Respect the beach's laws and regulations, pick up after yourself, don't damage the area's animals or sensitive coral reefs, and don't leave rubbish behind.

Wailea Beach offers the best Hawaiian beach experience because of its immaculate beaches, crystal-clear waves, and lavish facilities.

Whether you're searching for leisure, water activities, or just a peaceful place to soak up the sun, Wailea Beach provides a slice of paradise that will leave you with precious memories and a desire to visit Maui's breathtaking coastlines again.

Lahaina Historic District

A peek into the rich history and cultural legacy of the island may be found in Hawaii's Lahaina Historic District. It is located on the western shore of Maui. For lovers of history and the arts, and those who want to experience the real old Hawaii, this colorful area is a must-visit. It is full of charm and personality. The following details relate to the Lahaina Historic District.

History

Lahaina served as the Hawaiian Kingdom's capital from 1820 until 1845, and its influence on local history was profound. Due to its importance as a whaling port and a hub for worldwide commerce in fur and sandalwood, the town was a melting pot of cultures and influences.

Front Street
The Main Street that runs through the heart of Lahaina's Historic District is lined by lovely buildings that pay homage to the town's heritage. Today, it is a vibrant district to explore, with art galleries, boutiques, restaurants, and one-of-a-kind stores.

Square Banyan Tree
One of the most prominent features in the area is the Lahaina Banyan Court Park, which is home to the biggest banyan tree in the country. The area receives shade and aesthetic value from this massive tree, which was initially planted in 1873 and today covers more than an acre of ground.

The Lahaina harbor
From the busy Lahaina Harbor, visitors may go out on a range of ocean excursions, including snorkeling, whale viewing (during certain times of the year), sunset cruises, and

fishing charters. The harbor's nautical history enhances the district's charm.

Historical Buildings
The Lahaina Historic District is home to several well-preserved historic buildings, some of which are listed on the National Register of Historic Places. Notable sites include the Baldwin Home Museum, the Wo Hing Museum, the Old Lahaina Courthouse, and the Lahaina Jodo Mission.

Cultural Walk
The area is well known for having a vibrant art scene, with several galleries showing the works of local and foreign artists. Take part in cultural activities, art walks, and exhibits to experience Maui's artistic spirit.

The Nightlife

As the sun sets, Front Street comes to life with a lively nightlife. Enjoy luaus, live music, performances, and other occasions that celebrate Hawaiian entertainment and culture.

Whaling

The tradition of Lahaina's whaling industry permeates the neighborhood. The Wharf Cinema Center and the Lahaina Harbor provide visitors with a unique and educational experience since they may still hear the tales of the town's whaling heritage.

Cultural events

Throughout the year, Lahaina has a variety of cultural events that promote Hawaiian traditions in terms of music, dance, and handicrafts. The Lahaina Plantation Days Festival celebrates the area's rich plantation history each year.

Accessibility

It is simple to get to the Lahaina Historic District on foot, enabling tourists to explore its lovely streets in their own time. The district's hub is easily accessible because of the abundance of surrounding parking spaces.

Environmental Stewardship

As a historical and cultural resource, the district's past and surroundings must be preserved. Pay heed to any cautions or guidelines that may be posted, and support neighborhood efforts to preserve Lahaina's heritage.

The Lahaina Historic District, which is like stepping back in time, offers a chance to connect with Hawaii's interesting history while soaking up the dynamic present. By fusing historical buildings, creative expression, and cultural activities, Lahaina encourages you to immerse yourself in the essence of ancient Hawaii and the aloha spirit that still thrives in this enchanting coastal town.

Molokini Crater

Molokini Crater, a spectacular and unspoiled marine sanctuary off the southwest coast of Maui, Hawaii, offers an unrivaled snorkeling and diving experience. This volcanic crater is half underwater, full of marine life, and a must-see destination for nature enthusiasts and thrill seekers. The information below will tell you everything you need to know about Molokini Crater.

Geographical View

On the islet known as Molokini Crater, a previous volcanic outburst created a safe crescent-shaped basin. The crater is partly buried on its back, with its front exposed to the open ocean at a height of around 49 meters (160 feet) above sea level.

Marine Reserve Protection

Molokini Crater has been classified as a Marine Life Conservation District and a State Seabird Sanctuary to save its sensitive marine ecology and bird habitats. The seas around the crater are rich in vibrant marine life and provide excellent snorkeling and diving sites.

Snorkeling and scuba diving

The waters around Molokini crater are quiet and transparent, which makes them ideal for diving and snorkeling. Visitors may explore the colorful coral reefs, discover a plethora of tropical species, and possibly even stumble across dolphins, manta rays, or green sea turtles.

Underwater visibility

Off Molokini, there are moments when the underwater visibility may approach 150 feet (46 meters). Snorkelers and divers may completely immerse themselves in the spectacular marine environment and take in the diversity of aquatic life because of the outstanding visibility.

Tours with assistance

The majority of visitors to Molokini Crater take organized boat trips that depart from Maui's surrounding ports. Several tour operators provide morning and afternoon trips, together with snorkeling gear, safety training, and professional instructors to make the experience even better.

Accessibility

Despite being a popular tourist attraction, entrance to Molokini Crater is limited to save the area's fragile marine habitat. There are restrictions on how many people may visit the crater at once to save the underwater ecosystem.

Climate

The climate in and around Molokini Crater is warm and sunny, with temperatures in the mid-70s to mid-80s Fahrenheit (24-30°C). Put on comfortable swimwear, carry a towel, and don't forget sunscreen to protect yourself from the scorching Hawaiian heat.

Environment Stewardship

When snorkeling or diving in Molokini Crater, use responsible diving and diving practices to protect the marine ecosystem and coral reefs. Avoid touching or walking on coral and refrain from feeding or chasing marine creatures.

The Waters

Many tour operators and interpreters provide enlightening comments about marine life and the importance of conservation initiatives. Learn why it's critical to save this endangered marine sanctuary and how you can contribute to its preservation.

Other things to do

To offer a special and unforgettable experience, several trips combine visits to Molokini Crater with additional excursions, including stops at neighboring snorkeling areas like Turtle Town or pauses for whale viewing (seasonal).

It is possible to explore Hawaii's fascinating underwater environment and see the plethora of marine life that flourishes in this protected sanctuary by visiting Molokini Crater. Molokini's crystal-clear waters and variety of marine life provide a memorable experience that will leave you with irreplaceable memories of Maui's remarkable natural beauty, whether you're an experienced diver or a newbie snorkeler.

Maui Ocean Center

The Maui Ocean Center is a premier aquarium and marine life park located in Ma'alaea, Maui, Hawaii. It is a well-known area that showcases the variety of marine life found in the seas of Hawaii and offers tourists an interesting and instructive experience. You can get all the details about Maui Ocean Center right here.

Place and accessibility

The Maui Ocean Center is situated in the heart of Ma'alaea on Maui's south coast. There is lots of parking available, and driving there is simple. Due to its handy location, the center is an excellent spot to stop for tourists who are exploring the island.

The operation hours

Visitors may explore the exhibits and marine life at the Maui Ocean Center any day of the week. On the official website, you may find the most updated business hours as well as any forthcoming activities or events.

Exhibits & Displays

The aquarium has a variety of displays that showcase the marine life in the Pacific Ocean and Hawaii. View the sharks, rays, and other giant fish up close in the 750,000-gallon tank at the Open Ocean exhibit. Green sea turtles may be seen at the Turtle Lagoon, and the Living Reef exhibit has vibrant coral formations and tropical reef species.

Underwater Tunnel

One of the centerpieces of the Maui Ocean Center is the 54-foot-long acrylic tunnel that takes visitors through the Open Ocean exhibit. As you go down the tunnel, a variety of intriguing aquatic animals will surround you, giving the sensation that you are underwater.

Educational Programs
The Maui Ocean Center offers engaging displays and educational activities all day long. Learn about the creatures, their behaviors, and the importance of ocean conservation from marine biologists.

The aquatic life
For a more realistic experience, think about booking a Marine Animal Encounter. You may snorkel in the Open Ocean exhibit, swim with rays or sharks, go on a unique behind-the-scenes tour to learn more about the center's operations or do any of the other activities listed.

Sustainable Methods

The Maui Ocean Center is committed to using sustainable methods and safeguarding the environment. They run initiatives to decrease their environmental effect, promote marine conservation, and work with the local community.

Eating.

The facility offers on-site eating choices where you may eat while watching the picturesque Ma'alaea Harbor. Additionally, the Ocean Treasures gift store sells a variety of items with marine themes.

Family Settings

All of the interactive displays and events at the Maui Ocean Center are suitable for children and families. In this amazing environment, children may learn about the marvels of marine life and ocean conservation.

Photography Guidelines

Visitors are allowed to take photos and movies in most of the exhibitions. However, drones and flash photography are not permitted to safeguard the well-being of animals.

A visit to Maui Ocean Center offers a unique opportunity to see Hawaii's marine life up close without getting wet. There, it is simple to learn about the Pacific Ocean's abundant biodiversity and the need of safeguarding these vulnerable ecosystems. Whether you're going alone, with family, or in a group, Maui Ocean Center ensures a memorable and enlightening experience that highlights the beauty and mysteries of the ocean.

Wai'anapanapa State Park

The beautiful Wai'anapanapa State Park, which showcases the island's natural magnificence and historical value, is located on the northeastern coast of Maui. Wai'anapanapa State Park offers tourists a unique and immersive experience in the heart of Maui's untamable nature with its stunning black sand beach, historical lava caves, green surrounds, and dramatic shoreline. The information below will tell you all you need to know about Wai'anapanapa State Park.

The Beauty
The park's beautiful black sand beach was produced when ancient lava flows collided with the pounding waves of the Pacific Ocean. The unusual black sand, the deep lava cliffs, and the lush greenery all create a

remarkable contrast, making this a photographer's paradise.

The Culture
Wai'anapanapaa State Park is of the highest cultural importance to the Hawaiians. The place is known by the Hawaiian name "Wai'anapanapa," which means "glistening waters." It is believed that ancient Hawaiian monarchs used it as a holy sanctuary. The park is not only lovely but also rich in tradition and legend.

The Dark Sand Beach
Thee park's black sand beach is one of its main attractions. Due to the volcanic basalt that gives the beach's sheltered cove its distinctive hue, it is perfect for swimming and sunbathing. Keep an eye out for strong currents and waves beyond the cove since they might be dangerous for swimming.

Caves and Sea Arches

In Wai'anapanapa State Park, a network of fascinating sea caves formed by lava flows may be explored. Be amazed by the sea arches that the unrelenting sea has sculpted out of the rock as you explore the ancient lava tube caves, such as the Hana Lava Tube.

Hiking Trails

A variety of lovely hiking paths weave through lush tropical flora and along the rugged shoreline in the park. The most popular walk is the Pailoa Coastal Walk, which provides stunning views of the black sand beach and lava rocks.

Various Amenities and Picnic Areas

There are tidy picnic spots where visitors may dine while admiring the natural beauty of Wai'anapanapa State Park. There are bathrooms, showers, and parking facilities available for your convenience.

Camping

Camping is permitted at Wai'anapanapa State Park, providing visitors with a unique opportunity to take in the beauty and sounds of the Hawaiian environment. Make reservations as soon as you can since there are only a few spots available and permissions are required.

Accessibility

Even though most of the park's parts are accessible, some of the paths may have uneven terrain and be relatively difficult. The picnic spaces and wheelchair-accessible black sand beach allow everyone to take in the park's splendor.

Environmental Stewardship

Responsible tourism is crucial to preserving the vulnerable ecosystems in all Hawaii State Parks. Protect the rich marine and terrestrial life of Wai'anapanapa State Park by leaving no trace and only taking what you need.

Visits to Wai'anapanapa State Park provide the opportunity to take in Hawaii's pristine natural beauty and discover its rich cultural history. Whether you prefer to stroll along the coast, visit ancient lava caves, or just unwind on the black sand beach, Wai'anapanapa ensures a distinctive and enlightening experience that reflects the essence of Maui's captivating surroundings.

PART V: Activites and Entertainment

Beaches and Water Activities

Beaches

Maui, Hawaii's second-largest island, is recognized for its scenic and diverse shoreline. It provides a large selection of breathtaking beaches that are appropriate for different types of beachgoers. From golden beaches and blue oceans to secret coves and rough lava shorelines, every beach on Maui provides a unique and wonderful experience. Come along with me as I visit some of this tropical paradise's most attractive beaches.

The Ka'anapali beach

Ka'anapali Beach, one of Maui's most well-known and popular beaches, is located on the western coast of the island. Rich hotels, lively stores, and famous restaurants along a three-mile strip of glittering sand.

Ka'anapali Beach provides superb snorkeling at Black Rock, a well-known lava promontory at the northern end, as well as nightly cliff diving rituals, making it the perfect destination for families and couples seeking a blend of leisure and entertainment.

From the beach, watch the magnificent sunset as the sun sinks below the horizon, casting an eerie orange and purple glow over the sky.

Beach in Wailea.

Wailea Beach is located in the upscale resort area of Wailea and exudes refinement and serenity. The area's flawless white sand and calm, clear seas are perfect for swimming, sunning, and strolling. Wailea Beach offers a rich and opulent beach experience thanks to the world-class hotels and golf courses that surround it.

Reserve a cabana or beach umbrella for a day of complete leisure. Your every need will be met by the kind beach personnel, who will even give you a massage on the sand.

Ho'okipa Beach Park

At Ho'okipa Beach Park on Maui's north coast, the windsurfing and kitesurfing conditions are quite favorable. Due to the strong trade winds and consistent waves, it is a favorite with watersports watchers and participants. The beach is a well-known spot for seeing green sea turtles since they usually savor the sun on the sand there.

Admire breath-taking action images of this heart-pounding sport as skilled windsurfers and kiteboarders do amazing stunts on the waves.

The Makena Beach

Makena Beach, sometimes referred to as Big Beach, lives true to its name with its expansive length of golden sand that extends for about two miles. This secluded beach is a local favorite due to its natural beauty and excellent swimming conditions. At the northern end of Big Beach lies Little Beach, a no-clothes-required beach known for its bohemian feel and Sunday drum circles.

Climb the slope at the southern end of Big Beach for expansive views of the coastline and the fascinating crescent-shaped bay

The Kapalua Bay

Kapalua Bay, one of the nicest beaches in the world, is situated in the middle of the Kapalua Resort. It's a secluded cove and calm seas make it the perfect place for swimming and snorkeling since it has a rich underwater world filled with colorful fish and marine life. Keep an eye out for elegant green sea turtles swimming through the crystal-clear seas as you snorkel amid tropical fish and coral reefs.

Bay of Napili

Just north of Kapalua lies Napili Cove, a charming crescent-shaped cove with welcoming golden sands and swaying palm palms. This family-friendly beach is widely recognized for having excellent boogie boarding and body surfing conditions, making it a popular option for water sports aficionados.

Enjoy a beach picnic with local food while soaking up the sun and the laid-back vibe of Napili Bay.

Red Sand Kaihalulu Beach

Red Sand Beach, which is near Hana, is a hidden treasure that may be reached after a brief but strenuous climb. The beach's unusual reddish-black sand, cliffs, and surrounding lava rocks provide an exotic and remote ambiance for those looking for a more off-the-beaten-path encounter.

You'll be rewarded with a lovely, secluded area for relaxation provided you can handle the incline of the cliffside route to the beach.

Hamoa Beach

On Maui's eastern coast, not far from Hana, lies Hamoa Beach, a stunning crescent-shaped cove surrounded by lush greenery and swaying palm trees. Perfect for swimming, bodysurfing, and beachcombing, this beach has beautiful white sand, turquoise waves, and crystal-clear skies.

Wander down the coast at your leisure and explore the tidal pools at the eastern end. There may be some fascinating aquatic creatures to observe.

Honolulu Bay

Honolua Bay, on the northwest coast of Maui, is a refuge for divers and snorkelers. A startling diversity of marine life, as well as brilliant coral formations and schools of tropical fish, may be seen in this protected marine park.

Explore the underwater world by diving or snorkeling in the bay's crystal-clear waters, where you could be lucky enough to glimpse playful dolphins or even humpback whales during the winter.

Kanaha Beach

At Kanaha Beach Park, which is adjacent to Kahului Airport, locals take pleasure in windsurfing, kitesurfing, and beach camping. Shallow waters and regular trade winds provide ideal circumstances for learning to engage in watersports or for watching seasoned athletes show off their skills.

Experience: Enjoy a beachfront cookout as the sun sets over the West Maui Mountains while watching kites- and windsurfers dance over the waters.

Baldwin Beach

A popular beach for swimming, beachcombing, and picnics is Baldwin Beach Park. It is located at Paia on the north side of Maui. Visitors have lots of space to sprawl out and enjoy the sun and waves due to the beach's length.

Take a walk around the beachfront to see if you can find any kiteboarders or windsurfers surfing the waves.

Paako Beach

Pa'ako Beach or Makena Secret Beach, also known as Makena's Secret Beach, is a picturesque hidden treasure buried amid rich estates. Despite being rather far, the beach offers a tranquil escape with stunning views of the adjacent islands.

Experience: Track out this undiscovered treasure and enjoy the serenity while listening to the calm crashing of the waves.

Each of Maui's beaches provides a unique experience that showcases the island's diverse topography and unmatched natural beauty. They represent a rainbow of seaside joys. Every beach lover's dream comes true at Maui's beaches, which have everything from the upscale resorts of Wailea to the charming small-town atmosphere of Hana, from the exhilarating watersports of Ho'okipa to the peaceful tranquillity of Secret Beach. You'll surely leave Maui's beaches with wonderful memories of your stay there, whether you came for leisure, adventure, or watersports.

Other Water Activites

Maui is renowned for its crystal-clear seas, teeming marine life, and consistent trade winds, making it a water sports enthusiast's heaven. All skill levels may enjoy the broad variety of exhilarating water sports that Maui has to offer, from paddling a stand-up paddleboard or kayak or snorkeling and scuba diving to catching the perfect wave when surfing or windsurfing. Let's plunge in and explore the thrilling water activities that this aquatic haven has to offer:.

Snorkeling and scuba diving
The undersea environment of Maui is home to a wide variety of marine life that is both plentiful and colorful. Along with vivid tropical fish and beautiful sea turtles, snorkelers and scuba divers may see manta rays that are calm and majestic. The

destinations listed here are some of the best for scuba diving and snorkeling.

Molokini Crate is a volcanic crater that is only partly submerged and is well-known for its pristine waters and a variety of marine life, including reef sharks, eels, and schools of tropical fish.

On Maui's northwest coast lies Honolua Bay, a marine preserve that offers wonderful snorkeling and diving possibilities with a diversity of coral and fish species.

Olowalu, a lively coral reef on the west coast of Maui, is a haven for sea turtles and a variety of fish species. Kayak trips or boat cruises may take you there.

Wailea's Coral Gardens is a popular snorkeling spot because of the variety of marine life and vivid coral structures there.

Both novice and experienced surfers flock to the north and south coastlines of Maui because of its world-class surfing conditions. Due to its constant trade winds, the island is a windsurfing haven. These are popular surfing locations.

Strong waves and consistent trade winds make Ho'okipa Beach one of the best spots in the world for kiteboarding and windsurfing.

Honolua Bay: Located on Maui's northwest coast, this spot provides expert surfers with difficult waves in the winter.

Lahaina Breakwall: Longboarders and novices appreciate this site because it has gentler waves and a safe space for instruction.

Stand-Up Paddleboarding, or SUP

Using a steady board and stand-up paddleboarding (SUP), explore the seas of Maui. Here are a few popular SUP spots:.

On Maui's west coast, Olowalu is a tranquil, shallow cove that's wonderful for novices and a terrific site to observe sea turtles.

A quiet SUP location with calm waves and amazing marine life is Makena Landing in South Maui.
The beaches in Kihei are ideal for a leisurely paddle since they are close to the ocean and have quiet weather.

Kayaking and canoeing

Kayaking and canoeing allow you to leisurely explore Maui's secret coves and breathtaking coastline. Here are a few places where you can go kayaking and canoeing.

Explore the lava arches and sea caves in La Perouse Bay while kayaking Makena's craggy coastline.

Olowalu: Paddle the shores of this beautiful bay and explore the tranquil seas.

Hana: To enjoy the untamed beauty of Maui's eastern coast, go kayaking in the calm waters of Hana Bay or explore the sea caves adjacent to Waianapanapa State Park.

When participating in water activities in Maui, it is essential to put safety and environmental preservation first. Always follow the directions of qualified instructors or guides, put on the appropriate safety gear, and practice responsible tourism to protect the island's delicate marine ecosystems.
Whether you're looking for underwater exploration through snorkeling and scuba

diving, the rush of catching waves while surfing and windsurfing, or the peace of gliding along the water on a stand-up paddleboard or kayak, Maui offers a wide range of thrilling water activities that will leave you with priceless memories of your aquatic adventures in this paradise location.

Outdoor Adventures

The second-largest island in Hawaii, Maui, is a great destination for outdoor enthusiasts looking for adrenaline activities and opportunities to completely immerse themselves in the island's natural marvels. Numerous thrilling outdoor activities are available in Maui, such as horseback riding through the island's beautiful jungles, hiking to magnificent waterfalls, watching hypnotic humpback whales, and zipping through the air on zip lines. A handful of the most amazing outdoor activities that this tropical oasis has to offer are highlighted here.

Natural Hiking Trails

On Maui, there are a plethora of hiking paths that attract hikers of all skill levels and reward them with breathtaking panoramas and encounters with exotic flora and animals. Several popular hiking trails include:.

Hike through the strange environment of the Haleakala Crater in Haleakala National Park via the Sliding Sands Trail or the Pipiwai Trail to Waimoku Falls.

Iao Valley State Park: Explore the lush jungle paths that lead to the emerald-colored peak known as the Iao Needle, which is shrouded in mist.

Panorama views of the surrounding valleys and beaches are available from the Waihee Ridge Trail, which is somewhat challenging.

The Pipiwai Trail is located in Haleakala National Park's Kipahulu District and leads to the spectacular Waimoku Falls.

Waterfall Trips

On the island of Maui, there are numerous lovely waterfalls where falling waters create an ethereal atmosphere. You have to go on the waterfall trips listed below.

Twin Falls: From the Hana Highway, a short climb will take you to these magnificent waterfalls and swimming spots.

Visitors may cool themselves at the Seven Sacred Pools (Ohe'o Gulch), a feature of Haleakala National Park, after trekking the Pipiwai Trail.

Hana's Wailua Falls, a well-known roadside waterfall that flows powerfully soon after a rainstorm, is best seen at that time.

Makahiku Falls, a waterfall that charms hikers with its verdant surrounds, is located along the Pipiwai Trail.

Whale Watching

When humpback whales migrate to Hawaiian waters in December through April, Maui becomes a favored destination. People may come up close to these gentle giants and enjoy their playful activities, including breaching and slapping their tails, with the aid of whale-watching tours.

Trips using zip lines:
For those seeking an adrenaline rush, zip-lining tours provide a thrilling way to experience Maui's scenery. As you glide over lush valleys and through canopy treetops on one of the island's many zipline trips, you'll

get a birds-eye perspective of its natural beauty.

Horse Riding

To get a sense of traditional Hawaii, ride a horse across Maui's stunning scenery. Horseback riding trips through lush meadows, along coastal cliffs, and into secret valleys allow you to take in the natural beauty of the island while developing a particular bond with these gentle creatures.

When engaging in outdoor activities in Maui, it's critical to prioritize safety and adhere to responsible tourism standards. Respect the environment and heed the guidance of seasoned tour guides and operators for a great and sustainable trip.

From the exciting heights of zip-lining to the serene exploration of hiking paths, Maui provides a treasure trove of outdoor experiences that emphasize the island's natural grandeur. Whether you're seeking for heart-pounding activities or an opportunity to connect with nature, Maui's outdoor experiences provide a once-in-a-lifetime experience that will leave you with priceless memories of this tropical paradise.

Shopping in Maui

Art Galleries and Boutiques

Maui's vibrant art scene and boutique culture provide a fascinating shopping experience in addition to the usual souvenirs. With chic shops offering one-of-a-kind handmade products and contemporary galleries presenting the works of local artists, shopping in Maui transforms into an experience of artistic expression and creative inquiry. Whether you're an art fan, a design lover, or just seeking one-of-a-kind treasures, Maui's art galleries, and boutiques are guaranteed to capture your senses and leave you with priceless keepsakes of your island travels.

Art Galleries: Displaying a range of artistic genres, from cutting-edge modern works to traditional Hawaiian art, Maui's art galleries are a creative refuge. As soon as you step into these galleries, you'll be greeted with an astounding collection of paintings, sculptures, ceramics, and other fine art pieces that capture the island's natural beauty and cultural character. Some well-known art galleries in Maui are:.

A center for culture, the Hui No'eau Visual Arts Center (Makawao) organizes exhibits, seminars, and other activities to promote the creations of local and international artists.

Lahaina Galleries (Numerous sites): With a variety of sites on the island, Lahaina Galleries provides a vast selection of artwork by both local and international artists, including paintings, glass art, and sculptures.

Turnbull Fine Art (Paia): With a focus on modern art, Turnbull Fine Art exhibits stunning pieces created by well-known artists from throughout the globe and motivated by Maui's scenery and culture.

Shops: The handmade and locally produced items on offer at Maui's shops highlight the island's artistic skill and workmanship. Finding one-of-a-kind things that embody the character of the island is possible at these stores, from jewelry and clothes to home goods and health products. Here are a few cute stores to visit

The Pearl Butik
Local designers and artisans create cutting-edge clothing, accessories, and jewelry offered at Pearl Butik in Makawao.

Maui Hands: This collective store has various sites all around the island and sells a variety of goods manufactured there, including clothing, pottery, and glass and glassware.

Native Intelligence (Wailuku): Native Intelligence specializes in authentic Hawaiian artwork and cultural things and offers a variety of handmade goods and gifts that honor the island's past.

Paia Mercantile: it reflects the distinctive and artistic character of Paia town and includes apparel, jewelry, household products, and gifts that are inspired by the islands.

One of the most fulfilling elements of perusing Maui's art galleries and shops is realizing that your purchases are supporting local craftspeople and artists. By buying their creations, you help to support the island's thriving artistic community and contribute to the celebration and preservation of its unique cultural history.

Events & Art Walks: Maui's art galleries routinely participate in events and art walks that allow visitors to wander around a variety of galleries and interact with artists in person. Through these opportunities, you may engage with the local art community and get insight into the creative process.

Seeing Maui's art galleries and shops is an interesting and instructive experience that showcases the island's creative variety and inventiveness. Whether you're looking to add a special piece of art to your collection, discover a thoughtful gift, or simply want to immerse yourself in the beauty of Maui's cultural expressions, these artistic havens offer an exceptional shopping experience that will leave you inspired and connected to the spirit of the island.

Local Markets and Craft Fairs

On Maui, you may find a true gold mine of handmade items at local markets and craft fairs. These events provide a genuine and interesting shopping experience that lets you get to know the island's rich culture and talented craftsmen. Whether you're seeking one-of-a-kind gifts, local crafts, or farm-fresh fruit, these bustling markets give you a chance to experience the island's creative spirit and support the surrounding economy. Here are some justifications for why visiting Maui's local markets, from colorful farmers' markets to exciting artisan fairs, is a crucial component of your island vacation.

Handcrafted Artisans: At Maui's local markets and craft festivals, you may discover a broad range of handcrafted artwork that represents the island's rich cultural background. These unique works of art, which vary from deftly woven lauhala (pandanus) products to masterfully carved wooden artifacts, represent the histories and traditions of Hawaii's artists that have been handed down through the years.

Instead of buying generic souvenirs, look for one-of-a-kind items from local markets that wonderfully express the character of Maui. These keepsakes, which include handcrafted jewelry and pottery as well as unique paintings and prints, will help you remember the island's beauty long after your vacation.

Farmers' markets in Maui are a feast for the senses, with a plethora of fresh, locally produced vegetables, tropical fruits, and artisanal culinary items. Enjoy unique sweets like lilikoi (passion fruit) butter, Maui honey, and freshly baked coconut bread to experience the tastes of the island.

Cultural Immersion: At local markets and artisan shows, you may see firsthand the lively culture and way of life of Maui. Discover local goods, interact with friendly vendors, and take in the warm aloha atmosphere that pervades every corner of these lively markets.

Live Entertainment: A lot of local farmers' markets and craft fairs have live music and other forms of entertainment, which ups the festive vibe and makes shopping enjoyable for people of all ages.

Farm-to-Table Experience: Maui's farmers' markets provide a genuine farm-to-table experience by allowing you to directly communicate with local farmers and producers. Taste the difference that freshly picked food makes while appreciating sustainable methods that prioritize locally sourced components.

Support Local Businesses: You can contribute to the island's economy and foster a sense of community by directly supporting small businesses and independent craftsmen via your purchases at local markets and craft fairs.

Seasonal specials: Local markets on Maui often have seasonal specials, depending on the time of year. Every visit provides a unique range of goods that capture the many holidays and seasons, from tropical flowers to seasonal crafts.

DIY Workshops: A few craft markets and fairs offer DIY workshops where you can learn traditional crafts like weaving or creating lei, or you can even create your original piece of art to take home as a souvenir.

Local markets and artisan fairs are often held in picturesque villages and neighborhoods, providing an opportunity to explore lesser-known areas of Maui and discover off-the-beaten-path hidden treasures.

Shopping in Maui's local markets and craft fairs, then, is a satisfying and educational experience that goes beyond conventional retail therapy. On this trip of exploration and cultural immersion, you may come across one-of-a-kind treasures, interact with talented artists, and contribute to the island's dynamic community. You'll find that Maui's local markets are more than simply locations to purchase things; they are thriving centers of tradition, creativity, and the aloha spirit that contribute to the island's status as a genuinely one-of-a-kind travel destination. You'll discover that these markets are more than simply locations to make purchases as you look around the vibrant booths and exchange greetings with friendly traders.

Souvenirs to Bring Home

Maui has a lot to offer in terms of one-of-a-kind souvenirs that you may bring home with you thanks to its breathtaking beauty, vibrant culture, and welcoming people. Here is a selection of souvenirs, including tasty snacks, genuine Hawaiian crafts, and fashionable mementos, that reflect the essence of Maui and make your memories endure for a lifetime.

Handcrafted jewelry: Choose items made of Hawaiian pearls, sea glass, and jewels to accessorize with the beauty of the islands.

Look for works of art that are inspired by the island's seas and flora and animals.

Products of lauhala: Using leaves from the pandanus tree, lauhala is a traditional Hawaiian craft. Bring home accessories like hats, backpacks, tablecloths, or fans made from this complex and ecological material.

Local Art: To understand more about the island's booming art culture, see original paintings, prints, and sculptures created by local artists. Choose décor pieces that embody the colors and beauty of Maui to bring some sunshine into your home.

Hawaiian quilts: they are well known for their intricate designs and extensive histories. Bring home a quilt or a smaller quilted item like a wall hanging or pillow cover to give your décor a touch of Hawaiian history.

Play the ukulele in the Hawaiian way to reflect the spirit of aloha. Whether you're a musician or a collector, this little guitar-like instrument captures the soulful melodies of the islands.

Macadamia Nuts: Delicious macadamia nuts from Maui are a popular culinary keepsake. Choose from a range of tastes, including roasted and salted, chocolate- or honey-covered.

Hawaii's Kona coffee: This is a popular beverage because of its rich and smooth taste. So that you may awaken to a taste of the islands, grab a bag of this specialty coffee and bring it home.

Hawaiian made Dresses: Wear a stylish muumuu outfit with eye-catching island motifs or the classic Hawaiian aloha shirt.

These timeless outfits are perfect for adding a touch of tropical style.

Tropical Fruit Preserves: Savor the tastes of Maui's tropical fruits with these delectable jams, jellies, and preserves. If you want something unusual to eat, try guava or lilikoi (passion fruit).

Local Jewelry: Take in the delicate beauty of jewelry, home décor, and other items crafted from shell and coral. These objects give your surroundings a whiff of the attraction of the sea.

Hawaiian Music: Purchase a CD or digital download that combines both traditional Hawaiian music and contemporary island music to bring the seductive sounds of the islands into your house.

Hana Shirt: For fashion connoisseurs, a Hana shirt is a prized collectible. It's a classic Hawaiian button-up shirt with eye-catching designs added on.

Island-Themed novels: To truly immerse yourself in the culture and history of Maui, read novels on Hawaiian folklore, hula, surfing, or island cuisine.

Whether you're seeking unique décor, delectable sweets, or traditional crafts, Maui souvenirs provide priceless reminders of your island vacation. These mementos provide you a chance to treasure Maui's natural grandeur, rich culture, and welcoming attitude long after you've said goodbye to the island.

PART VI: Eating

Traditional Hawaiian Cuisine

A reflection of the numerous civilizations that have formed the islands throughout time is seen in Hawaii's unique culinary legacy. Traditional Hawaiian cuisine, commonly known as "local food," mixes ingredients from Polynesian, Asian, and Portuguese cultures to produce a delicious combination of tastes and textures.

Here is a selection of mouthwatering traditional Hawaiian foods, featuring juicy meats cooked in imu (subterranean oven), tangy tropical fruits, and unusual seafood dishes.

Imu: It is sea salt-seasoned, slow-cooked, then wrapped with ti leaves. The main course during Hawaiian feasts is the kalua pig. The final product is tender, delicious, and smokey.

Lomi: Fish Lomi Salmon that has been sliced uncooked, tomatoes, onions, salt, and a dash of citrus make up this simple side dish

Poke: Raw fish, mainly ahi tuna, is prepared into this renowned Hawaiian snack, by marinating it in soy sauce, sesame oil, and other spices. Then, seaweed, onions, and chili peppers are placed on top.

Poi: A starchy, somewhat sour side dish prepared from mashed taro root that is a staple of Hawaiian cuisine and is often served with many traditional meals.

Lau Lau: A delicate and savory dish comprised of pork, fish, or chicken wrapped in taro leaves and steamed or cooked in an imu.

Dhupia: Popular Hawaiian desserts like the mouthwatering coconut pudding, regularly served during luaus and other special occasions.

Spam musubi: To make the well-known snack, a slice of grilled Spam is put on a block of rice and wrapped in nori (seaweed), drawing inspiration from the Japanese culture of the island.

Loco Moco: This substantial local staple consists of rice covered in flavorful brown gravy and topped with a hamburger patty, a fried egg, and cheese.

Rice meal: A typical plate meal consists of two scoops of rice, one scoop of macaroni salad, and a protein (such as teriyaki chicken, kalbi ribs, or lau lau). It is a tasty dish that is commonly offered as a convenient and satisfying choice.

Ono: Popular in Hawaiian cooking, ono (also known as wahoo) is a fish that is commonly grilled or eaten raw. It is recognized for both its sensitive texture and subtle taste.

L'au Stew: Taro leaves, coconut milk, spices, and a range of meats (usually chicken, hog, and beef) are combined to create this delectable stew. The outcome is a filling and cozy meal.

Pipikaula: Made from thinly sliced, marinated beef that has been dried out before being skillfully grilled, pipikaula is a Hawaiian take-on beef jerky.

Malasadas: Malasadas are fried doughnuts coated in sugar that are a wonderful dessert relished at festivals and other occasions. They were popularized by Portuguese immigrants.

Coconut Shrimp: A popular appetizer or main meal with dipping sauces, these crispy shrimp are wrapped in shredded coconut.

Huli chicken: it is a grilled chicken marinated in a sweet and savory marinade that is often served on a rotisserie.

Whether you're enjoying a plate lunch on the beach, eating at a local restaurant, or attending a l'au, these well-known dishes offer a culinary experience that will leave you craving more of Hawaii's delectable tastes.

Popular Local Dishes

Lunch Plate: The plate lunch is a local favorite and typically consists of two scoops of white rice, one scoop of macaroni salad, and your choice of protein, such as teriyaki chicken, kalua pig, or garlic shrimp. This hearty and enjoyable lunch offers a sample of Hawaii's many culinary traditions.

Poke: The well-known Hawaiian meal known as poke is made with diced raw ahi tuna or salmon that has been marinated in soy sauce, sesame oil, and other ingredients. Poke is a popular appetizer or entrée that is flavorful and light and typically paired with rice.

Spam musubi, a common snack or fast meal, a slice of grilled Spam is put on a block of rice and wrapped with nori (seaweed). This delectable snack, which draws inspiration from Japanese onigiri, highlights the blending of cultures in Hawaii.

Loco Moco: Using white rice as the basis, hamburger patties, fried eggs, and copious amounts of robust brown gravy on top, loco moco is a filling local cuisine. This basic comfort dish can satisfy any hunger.

Shave Ice: A refreshing dessert perfect for Hawaii's hot environment, shave ice is made of finely shaved ice that has been flavored with syrup and is usually topped with ice cream or sweetened condensed milk. Popular tastes include li hing mui and tropical fruits from the area.

Malasadas: They are deep-fried, sugar-coated doughnuts with Portuguese influences. These tasty sweets are well-liked at festivals and local bakeries.

Saimin: A noodle soup with Chinese and Japanese origins, saimin often features char siu (barbecued pork) along with green onions, fishcakes, and egg noodles in a delicious broth.

Poi: as mentioned before, it is made from mashed taro root, this Hawaiian classic has a unique texture and a pleasantly acidic taste. It is commonly served as an accompaniment or as a component of a l'au feast.

Kalbi ribs: they are short ribs that have been marinated in a delicious marinade with a touch of sweetness and then grilled to perfection. These tasty and tender ribs are served often at neighborhood barbecue establishments.

Lau lau is a meal composed of pork, fish, or chicken wrapped in ti leaves and cooked in an imu (underground oven) or steaming. The outcome is a delicious and delicate delicacy.

Pipikaula: A chewy, savory snack resembling beef jerky, pipikaula is made from thinly sliced, marinated beef that has been dried, grilled, or pan-fried.

Manapua: Another delicacy with Chinese culinary roots, Managua is a steamed bun stuffed with delicious pork, char siu, or other ingredients. Nearby bakeries or dim sum restaurants commonly carry these portable delicacies.

Haupia: a delectable coconut pudding from Hawaii, is made with coconut milk, sugar, and cornstarch. a typical sweet dish offered during luaus and other occasions.

Garlic Shrimp: This mouthwatering seafood recipe, which was inspired by North Shore cuisine, combines luscious shrimp with garlic, butter, and seasonings to create an irresistible meal.

These well-known local dishes highlight the vivid and varied tastes of Hawaii by incorporating ethnic influences to create a culinary tapestry that satisfies both residents and visitors. Every dish, from savory plate lunches to sweet save ice, celebrates the rich tradition of the island and the availability of fresh ingredients that give Hawaii's food its sinfully unique flavor.

Fine Dining Restaurants

Mama's Fish House: A famous seafood restaurant with a spectacular beachfront setting, Mama's Fish House is well-known for its fresh, locally caught fish and other Hawaiian delights. It is a great option for special events because of the attentive service and exquisite environment. The catch of the day is included on the daily changing menu.

Kapalua Merriman's
A farm-to-table restaurant in Hawaii, Merriman's takes pleasure in serving food made with organic, regional products. It may be found within the Kapalua Resort. Diners may enjoy breathtaking views of the Pacific Ocean's sunset while indulging in inventive meals inspired by the island's wealth.

The Lahaina Grill

Lahaina Grill, located in the town's core, offers a posh dining experience with a variety of contemporary American dishes. The quiet ambiance of the award-winning restaurant is perfect for a celebration or a romantic evening.

Humuhumunukunukuapua

The luxury Polynesian food is served in the Humuhumunukunukuapua'a restaurant of the Grand Wailea resort, which is suitably named after the state fish of Hawaii. Visitors may savor Pacific Rim delicacies in open-air bungalows with thatched roofs that overlook a peaceful lake.

Morimoto

This upmarket restaurant is run by famous chef Masaharu Morimoto and serves food with a combination of Japanese and Western ingredients. Fresh fish and premium ingredients are highlighted in the beautiful and creative gastronomic adventure offered by the Morimoto Maui restaurant.

Japengo

Inside the Hyatt Regency Maui Resort, there is a restaurant called Japengo that serves contemporary Pacific Rim cuisine with a concentration on sushi and fresh fish. Diners may enjoy inventive meals and handcrafted drinks while admiring breathtaking ocean vistas.

Ko (Wailea)

The food of Ko, a farm-to-table restaurant within the Fairmont Kea Lani resort, is influenced by the island's rich cultural history. The exquisite design and outdoor setting of the restaurant provide a serene and pleasant ambiance.

The Mill House

This is housed in the Maui Tropical Plantation, acknowledges Hawaii's agricultural wealth by serving food that is locally sourced and in-season. The dining area is surrounded by quiet gardens and a lagoon, creating a gorgeous scene.

The Gannon's

It offers a refined dining experience with a diverse cuisine of Hawaiian and foreign tastes, and it boasts a view of the Wailea Gold Golf Course. Sunset views from the restaurant's gorgeous outdoor patio make for the ideal after-dinner treat.

Nick's Seafood Market

The Fairmont Kea Lani Hotel is home to Nick's Fishmarket, which specializes in offering only the finest steaks and seafood. The exquisite atmosphere and comprehensive wine selection make it the ideal choice for a refined dining experience.

Ka'ana Kitchen

In the Andaz Maui at Wailea Resort, Ka'ana Kitchen offers farm-to-table cuisine with an emphasis on locally produced products. Due to the restaurant's distinctive family-style dining style, customers may enjoy a range of Cuisines.

The Humble Market Kitchin

Famous chef Roy Yamaguchi created the Humble Market Kitchin, which mixes Hawaiian, Asian, and European ingredients. The sleek and contemporary setting offers a welcoming environment for appreciating delectable cuisine.

Mauka Makai

The Mauka Makai restaurant at The Westin Nanea Ocean Villas pays homage to Hawaiian culture and cuisine while giving it a modern twist.

Diners may enjoy ocean vistas while they try delicacies that are influenced by the island's lengthy history.

Ferraro's Bar e Ristorante.

Inside the Four Seasons Resort Maui at Wailea, Ferraro's offers a genuine Italian dining experience. Customers may enjoy meals created using fresh, local ingredients while enjoying a view of Wailea Beach.

The Pacific'O.

Being close to the coast, it adopts a farm-to-table concept with an emphasis on sustainable techniques. The cuisine offers organic foods, fresh seafood, and a sizable wine selection.

The K Restaurant

Fairmont Kea Lani resort displays the varied gastronomic traditions from Hawaii's plantation history. There are meals from Chinese, Filipino, Japanese, Korean, Portuguese, and other cuisines on the menu.

Pulehu

Pulehu is a relaxed eatery that offers a warm fireplace, outside dining, and Italian cuisine with a Hawaiian flair. The cuisine includes grilled meats, fresh seafood, and classic pasta dishes.

The Pineapple Grill.

At the Pineapple Grill, a posh eatery inside the Kapalua Resort, modern Hawaiian food is provided in a warm environment. The cuisine offers locally produced products coupled with a blend of Asian and Pacific Rim tastes.

Each of these great dining restaurants in Maui welcomes visitors to revel in the delicacies of the island while surrounded by its beautiful natural beauty. Whether you're seeking exquisite foreign tastes, contemporary fusion cuisine, or classic Hawaiian cuisine, Maui's wide and great dining scene is likely to please even the pickiest palette.

PART VII: Accommodation & Transportation

Luxury Resorts

On Maui, which is known for its magnificent beaches and natural landscape, you can find a variety of luxury resorts that represent the height of elegance and first-rate service. These opulent hotels provide their guests with a tranquil retreat where they may indulge in first-rate facilities, great meals, and unique activities. If you're seeking the ultimate hideaway and a touch of luxury for a memorable trip, think about staying at one of Maui's lavish resorts. Below is a list of some of the island's most lavish luxury resorts.

The Four Seasons Resort in Wailea

Hidden along Wailea Beach, the Four Seasons Resort Maui is a tropical haven. Guest amenities include expansive rooms with private lanais, lavish spa treatments, award-winning restaurants, and a variety of recreational pursuits including golfing and snorkeling.

There is a Ritz-Carlton in Kapalua.
On Maui's beautiful northwest coast, The Ritz-Carlton, Kapalua provides a serene and elegant getaway. A world-class spa, direct access to the beach, elegant bedrooms and suites with views of the ocean or gardens, two championship golf courses, and the resort's other amenities are all available.

The Andaz Maui.
Modern and chic, The Andaz Maui at Wailea Resort is a refuge that personifies modern luxury. With its magnificent suites, cascading infinity pools, beachside cabanas, and excellent dining selections, this resort offers a dynamic and affluent environment.

The Montage Bay.

The luxurious residential-style accommodations at The Montage Kapalua Bay, which is set on the picturesque Kapalua Bay, provide spacious living areas and fully equipped kitchens. For visitors' comfort, there is a serene spa and farm-to-table eating.

The Grand Wailea.

The Grand Wailea is famed for its expansive grounds and ornate pools and oozes majesty and elegance. The resort provides stylish bedrooms and suites, a 20,000-square-foot spa, a selection of eating establishments, and a water park that is suitable for both adults and children.

The Hotel Kea Lani.

Only suites with private lanais and segregated living rooms are available at the beachside refuge which is the Fairmont Kea Lani. Visitors may choose from a wide range of culinary choices, spa treatments, and cultural events.

The Travaasa

It provides a quiet and distinctive location, is located in the remote and lush village of Hana. The region offers visitors a chance to relax, engage in cultural activities, and take in the beauty of Maui's eastern coast.

The Relais & Châteaux Hotel

The adults-only hotel Hotel Wailea offers a quiet, boutique setting. With spacious apartments, personal plunge pools, and expansive ocean views, this resort provides a sumptuous and serene getaway.

The Hyatt Regency Resort

On Ka'anapali Beach, the Hyatt Regency Maui Resort and Spa provides a breathtaking tropical environment. The resort's renowned spa, the beautiful grounds, and the pools can all be enjoyed by guests, who may even take part in a traditional luau.

Each of these luxurious Maui resorts offers a distinct and distinctive experience, making your journey to paradise memorable. Whether you're seeking for opulent leisure, thrilling experiences, or fine cuisine, these resorts are designed to exceed your expectations and help you create lifelong memories.

Boutique Hotels

Relais and Châteaux

This small hotel for adults only offers a quiet sanctuary on Maui's southern shore. The spacious apartments include private lanais and plunge pools, and guests may enjoy stunning ocean views from these areas. The hotel's dedicated service, renowned cuisine, and soothing spa treatments make it a fantastic choice for a romantic trip.

Lumeria Makawao

The holistic retreat and boutique hotel Lumeria Maui is hidden away amid lush gardens and rolling hills. There is farm-to-table eating, yoga, and health activities, and a tranquil setting that promotes relaxation and regeneration.

The Paia Inn

The charming hamlet of Paia is home to the Paia Inn Hotel, which offers a boutique experience only steps from Maui's North Shore beaches. The hotel is popular with tourists seeking a relaxed seaside getaway due to its stylish accommodations, convenient access to nearby shops and restaurants, and kind service.

Hotel Wailea.

It is set on a hillside with views of the Pacific Ocean and provides a stylish and sumptuous boutique stay. For a tranquil retreat, the hotel provides large suites and rooms with ocean views, a soothing spa, great cuisine, and an adults-only pool.

Ka'anapali Beach Hotel.

The Ka'anapali Beach Hotel is known as "Maui's Most Hawaiian Hotel" because it personifies the spirit of aloha. With its small accommodations, cultural programs, and simple access to the well-known Ka'anapali Beach, the boutique-style hotel offers a pleasant combination of authenticity and practicality.

The Plantation Inn.

The Inn is located in the city's historic district, exudes the grace and allure of a bygone period. French-inspired cuisine is served at this quaint restaurant, which also has a pool, green courtyard, and elegant rooms in a boutique hotel.

Budget-Friendly Lodgings

The Hawaiian island of Maui, which is well-known for its luxurious resorts and high-end lodgings, also provides a wide range of inexpensive lodging options that nonetheless provide comfort and convenience. Whether you're a backpacker, a budget traveler, or simply trying to save costs on housing, these options may accommodate a variety of interests and allow you to experience Maui's charm on a shoestring budget.

Hostels

Hostels are a good option for visitors on a tight budget searching for inexpensive shared housing. Many hostels on the island of Maui provide dormitory-style accommodations with shared amenities in well-known areas including Lahaina and Wailuku. Common rooms, kitchens, and social activities are commonly provided by hostels, promoting a vibrant and friendly atmosphere for tourists to socialize.

Vacation Rentals

These include condominiums, flats, and cottages are an economical option for families or groups of friends. These hotels usually provide kitchens and laundry facilities, providing visitors with the convenience of a home away from home. There are several vacation homes close to Maui's breathtaking beaches and tourist attractions.

Motels

On Maui, several cheap hotels and motels provide comfortable accommodations at affordable prices. Because they typically include standard facilities like free Wi-Fi, parking, and continental breakfasts, these motels are a logical choice for travelers on a small budget.

Camping

For visitors on a tighter budget, Maui's campsites provide an unparalleled opportunity to see nature up close. State parks with camping spaces and access to hiking routes include Haleakala and Wai'anapanapa.

Home sharing & Airbnb.

Airbnb and other home-sharing sites provide a variety of affordably priced choices for lone travelers and small groups. These hotel alternatives, which range from private rooms in private homes to lovely guesthouses, may provide a true sense of local life in Maui.

Breakfast Inns.

On the Hawaiian island of Maui, bed & breakfasts provide unique and reasonably priced accommodation. These charming lodgings typically provide breakfast for a delectable start to the day before exploring the island's attractions.

Eco-Lodges

Tourists who are concerned about the environment may stay in one of Maui's eco-lodges for a reasonable price. These lodgings prioritize environmental principles while offering unusual and serene surroundings to the outdoors.

Staycations

Keep an eye out for specials and staycation deals from nearby hotels and resorts. When last-minute deals or seasonal discounts provide exceptional value for money, it is possible to enjoy a more sumptuous stay without having to pay a high price tag.

Group discounts

If you are traveling in a group or with a family, think about asking for discounts on lodgings. Since many accommodations provide reduced prices for bigger groups, it is an economical option for shared costs.

Off-season Travels

Off-seasonn or shoulder travel might result in considerable hotel discounts. Because rates are often cheaper and there are fewer visitors around, you may take your time and appreciate the island's splendor.

When planning your inexpensive Maui vacation, keep in mind that these accommodations still provide plenty of opportunities to explore the island's breathtaking beaches, engage in cultural activities, and experience the welcoming atmosphere that makes Maui such a well-liked travel destination for everyone.

Transportation

Making the most of your vacation while seeing the beautiful island of Maui requires that you be aware of your transportation choices. No matter what you're seeking for in a mode of transportation—comfort, flexibility, or the opportunity to take in the island's beauty—Mauri provides a range of choices to meet your requirements. You can fully comprehend island transportation after reading the following information:.

Car Rentals

Renting a vehicle is the most common and practical method to see Maui. Many well-known automobile rental companies operate on the island and provide a variety of cars to meet your demands and the size of your party. If you possess a vehicle, you are free to explore Maui's undiscovered attractions, stunning drives like the route to Hana, and the well-known, winding route to Haleakala's peak.

Public Transit.
The island of Maui's public transportation system, the Maui Bus, offers an affordable means of getting about. The buses cover major thoroughfares, well-known tourist attractions, and commercial centers. Even while it takes longer than driving, it's still more inexpensive for individuals without a vehicle.

Ride-sharing services
Using well-known ride-sharing services like Uber and Lyft in Maui provides an alternative to traditional taxis. These services are particularly helpful for short excursions or when you wish to avoid parking and driving in crowded locations.

Biking

For environmentally aware travelers and outdoor lovers, biking is a fantastic way to experience Maui. Thanks to the many rental businesses that provide bicycles for hire, you may go on beautiful bike rides along the island's attractive coastline pathways or across its lush countryside.

Scooters and Mopeds

Using a scooter or moped to explore Maui's smaller villages and picturesque places is fun and efficient. Remember that you need a driver's license that is currently valid and a helmet to operate these vehicles.

Walking

If you're staying in a town like Lahaina, Paia, or Kihei, think about strolling to neighboring attractions, restaurants, and beaches. While wandering, you may take in the beauty and culture of the island at your speed.

Guided tours

The guided tours that are offered in Maui include adventure tours, bike tours, and van excursions, to name a few. When you take a tour, you can relax and take it all in as a professional guide tells you about the natural beauty, history, and culture of Maui.

Ferries

If you wish to visit the surrounding islands of Molokai and Lanai, ferries travel from Maui to those locations. The boat excursions provide beautiful scenery and an opportunity to discover each island's unique character.

By Air

If time is of the essence and you need to travel longer distances fast, flying between islands is an option. Island hopping is made easier by flights to neighboring Hawaiian islands from Maui's Kahului Airport (OGG).

Navigating Maui's many modes of transportation is not too difficult and each one has its advantages. Whether you prefer the freedom of a rental vehicle, the cost-effectiveness of public transportation, or the guided experiences of excursions, you'll discover the perfect method to explore the wonder and enchantment of Maui, assuring a satisfying and unforgettable island journey.

PART VIII:
Communication & Photography

Photographer's Tips

Thanks to Maui's gorgeous scenery and lively culture, photographers have endless opportunities to create spectacular and memorable photos. Follow this photographic advice, whether you're using a DSLR or a smartphone, to get the most out of your stay on the island:.

During Maui's golden hours, immediately after dawn and before sunset, when the soft, warm light spreads a wonderful atmosphere over the island, make the most of your visit. Photographers may capture stunning vistas, silhouettes, and portraits at this time of day.

Make your research: Before starting your photographic trip, do some research and check out suitable sites. You can efficiently plan your pictures if you know where to go, whether you're shooting in the lush Hana rainforests, the rugged North Shore, or the gorgeous Haleakala.

Permissions: Ask for permission before taking images of individuals or at private or religious locations to respect others and adhere to regional customs. Be mindful of any regulations since certain places can have limitations on taking photographs.

Beach photography: it is encouraged by the island's scenic coastline, but bear in mind that your equipment has to be waterproof to avoid damage from sand and water. Invest in waterproof camera coverings or use waterproof housing to protect your equipment.

Wildlife photography: Maui is home to a wide diversity of birds and marine life. If you want to get up close and personal with whales, sea turtles, and seabirds in their native environments, bring a telephoto lens or a camera with a good zoom.

Underwater photography: Invest in a top-notch waterproof camera or housing for your existing camera if you want to explore Maui's underwater environment. By snorkeling or scuba diving, you may get images of vivid coral reefs and colorful creatures.

Framing: Use the rule of thirds to frame your photographs and position your subject or horizon along intersecting lines. Using this method, a pleasing and well-balanced picture is created.

Long Exposure: To capture beautiful waterfalls or tranquil ocean waves, try long exposure photography at dawn or night. Use a tripod to keep your camera stable.

Edit With Care: While retouching might make your images better, try to keep Maui's natural beauty intact. Avoid employing too many filters or effects to maintain the scene's realism.

Connecting with locals

Your journey will be more interesting and richer if you meet locals.
Follow these recommendations and the aloha attitude to mingle with the locals.

Learn words like "Aloha" (hello), "Mahalo" (thank you), and "Ohana" (family) to become proficient in the language. It shows respect for the island's way of life to use these terms.

Join community gatherings, festivals, or hula performances to get a taste of the island's traditions. The neighborhood is pleased to share its history, and your involvement shows that you care.

Supporting neighborhood businesses may be done in a variety of ways, including dining at nearby eateries, shopping at small retailers, and purchasing goods created locally. Putting money into the neighborhood economy fosters a deeper feeling of community.

Show respect and civility to everyone you come into contact with. Smiling and saying "aloha" are simple yet honest ways to build connections with people.

Talk to the people and carefully consider the suggestions they provide. Their expertise can help you discover undiscovered treasures and unique experiences.

Participate in community service initiatives or beach clean-ups to give back to the island and get to know residents who are committed to maintaining Maui's beauty.

To better comprehend Hawaii's traditions, research the history and cultural practices of the state. Understanding the local culture encourages the development of meaningful bonds.

Creating Lasting Memories

By following the recommendations below, you may create priceless experiences that will last you a lifetime and leave a lasting image of Maui's beauty and allure.

Live in the Present: Occasionally disconnect from your devices and enjoy everything that Maui has to offer. Enjoy the island's views, sounds, and tastes while savoring the air of the lake.

Keep a trip diary: In your trip diary, you may record your daily thoughts, emotions, and experiences. You can retain and recall the feelings you had while visiting Maui by keeping a vacation diary.

Print Your Photos: While retaining tangible records of the past may be very touching, printing photos may feel antiquated in the digital era. Create a photo book or frame your favorite pictures to display them in your house.

Do something new: like go surfing, go to a hidden waterfall, or attend a traditional luau, to get out of your comfort zone.

Share Your Experiences: Whether via a travel blog, social media, or discussions with friends and family, sharing your Maui experiences allows you to relive the trip and inspires others to visit the island.

Gratitude: Practice Being Thankful by giving thought to the gifts and beauty you see in Maui each day. As you cultivate thankfulness, your appreciation for the island's offerings and your time there will increase.

Plan Your Return: Instead of saying goodbye to Maui, plan your next adventure. You'll be drawn back to the island by its charm for further exploration and treasured experiences.

Useful Phrases in Hawaiian

Your trip to Maui will be more enjoyable if you can communicate with the locals by learning a few Hawaiian terms and phrases. Even though English is widely spoken across the islands, respect for the local language and customs may be seen in the usage of these everyday Hawaiian idioms. To embrace the aloha spirit, learn to use these terms.

"Aloha," the most famous Hawaiian term, is pronounced "ah-loh-hah" and has the meanings "hello," "goodbye," and "love." It denotes a welcoming and kind disposition.

Say "mahalo" (pronounced "mah-hah-loh") to express your gratitude.

E Komo Mai is a salutation or invitation that is pronounced: "eh koh-moh my." It is a salutation or an invitation to enter.

Ohana, pronounced "oh-hah-nah," is Hawaiian meaning "family." In Hawaiian culture, the term "ohana" refers to close friends as well as blood relatives.

The Hawaiian word Maika'i, which is pronounced "my-kah-ee," means "good" or "excellent." Use it to praise something or to show appreciation.

The phrase "pau hana," which means "quitting time" or "happy hour," is used to indicate the conclusion of a workday or workweek.

A Hui Hou, which sounds like "until we meet again" (ah hoo-ee-hoh), is a Chinese goodbye. It's a heartfelt way to part ways.

You may be familiar with the term "Mele Kalikimaka" from a well-known Christmas carol. Meh-leh kah-lee-kee-mah-kah is the correct pronunciation.

"Merry Christmas," it says.

When wishing someone a "Happy Birthday," say "Hau'oli La Hanau" (how-oh-lee lah hah-now).

"E Ola Pono" (pronounce it "eh oh-lah poh-no") is a Hawaiian adage that translates to "live well" or "be healthy." It's a method to convey your warmest wishes for their well-being.

The ancient Hawaiian benediction Ke Akua Pu a Hui Hou means "May God Bless You Until We Meet Again."

Students or learners are referred to as "haumna" (pronounced "how-mah-nah") in educational circumstances.

Kkua (koh-koo-ah) is the Hawaiian word meaning "help" or "assistance". Anytime you want help, you must say "kkua."

Nani's (nah-nee) meaning is "beautiful" or "pretty." Use it to highlight the stunning landscape of Maui.

"Crazy" or "foolish" are the meanings of the fun phrase "pupule" (poo-poo-leh). When humorously describing something strange or entertaining.

Remember that learning and using these terms and expressions will not only make your stay in Maui more enjoyable but will also make you feel more at home among the natives. By using these useful expressions, you may improve your vacation to Maui and interact with the people more effectively. They will be touched by your attempts to understand and utilize their language and culture.

Other Hawaiian Islands

Maui's attraction is evident, but Hawaii is a treasure trove of unique islands, each with its beauty and cultural depth. By embarking on a journey to discover other Hawaiian islands, one has the opportunity to encounter a range of topographies, traditions, and experiences. From the congested cities of Oahu to the wild wildness of Kauai and the stunning mountains of the Big Island, each island has a distinct history to offer. Here is a guide to help you plan your tour of these attractive places

Oahu

Oahu, often known as the "Gathering Place," is the island with the highest population in Hawaii. It is also where Honolulu, the state's capital, is situated. Here, you'll find a thriving combination of urban life and scenic beauty.

Visit well-known places like Pearl Harbor and the USS Arizona Memorial, as well as historical sites like Iolani Palace and Waikiki Beach. Outdoor enthusiasts may enjoy a pleasant trek at the Diamond Head State Monument while taking in breathtaking views of the island's coastline. Don't forget to savor Oahu's varied culinary offerings and savor the island's vivacious culture by going to regional festivals and witnessing hula performances.

Kauai

Kauai, sometimes known as the "Garden Isle," is a verdant paradise with plenty of untouched beauty. To explore the breathtaking Na Pali Coast, use a boat, or a helicopter, or go on a stroll along the Kalalau Trail. Discover Waimea Canyon, the "Grand Canyon of the Pacific," and its stunning landscapes. If you're a movie fan, take a tour of famous shooting sites, such as "Jurassic

Park" and "Avatar."Because of its tranquility and isolated appeal, Kauai is the ideal holiday destination for individuals seeking a quiet retreat in nature.

Hawaiian Big Island.

The Island of Hawaii, commonly referred to as the "Big Island," is the largest and most recent of the Hawaiian islands. Its diverse environments vary from lush rainforests to barren deserts, and the Kilauea and Mauna Loa volcanoes are located there. Explore Hawaii Volcanoes National Park to see the force of devastation and rebirth firsthand. Take in the stars from Maunakea, one of the top astronomy observatories in the world. The Big Island is known for its world-class snorkeling spots, Kona coffee, and an abundance of marine life.

Molokai

Molokai offers a true glimpse into the history of Hawaii because of its slower pace of life and close ties to its indigenous culture. Learn about Father Damien's ministering to Hansen's disease patients at Kalaupapa National Historical Park. On Molokai's eastern side, see the ancient Hawaiian fishponds and take a trek along the magnificent sea cliffs of the Pali Coast. On this serene island, visitors may really and profoundly enjoy the Hawaiian culture and natural beauty.

Lanai

Lanai, sometimes known as "Pineapple Island," is a tranquil sanctuary that is far away.

Despite its small size, Lanai is home to lavish resorts, stunning beaches, and opportunities for off-road adventures. Take a guided jeep excursion to view Lanai's untamed interior, relax on the immaculate Hulopoe Beach, or visit the Garden of the Gods to witness the strange rock formations.

Niihau
Niihau, the "Forbidden Island," is privately owned and only gets sporadic access by the general public. There is a tiny community that still speaks Hawaiian and lives a traditional lifestyle. Even though it is often not permitted to enter Niihau, scenic flights or boat cruises let you take in the island's splendor from a distance.

You'll learn that each of Hawaii's other islands offers a unique perspective on the state's captivating tapestry of geology, culture, and history when you visit them. Whether you're seeking adventure, leisure, or a stronger connection to Hawaii's past, these islands are eager to share their charm with you. Remember to embrace the aloha spirit, show respect for the environment and local culture, and relish every moment as you set off on a memorable tour across paradise's numerous beauties.

Made in the USA
Middletown, DE
29 October 2023

41575808R00108